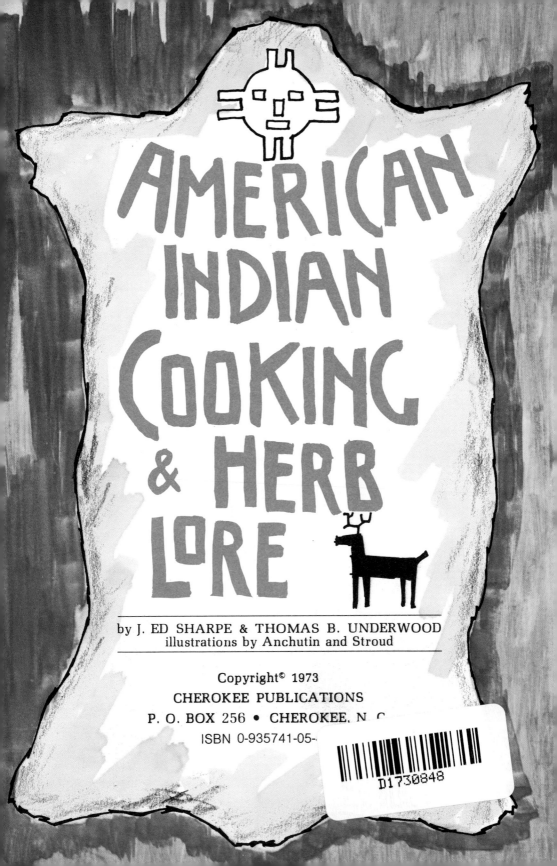

AMERICAN INDIAN COOKING & HERB LORE

by J. ED SHARPE & THOMAS B. UNDERWOOD
illustrations by Anchutin and Stroud

Copyright© 1973
CHEROKEE PUBLICATIONS
P. O. BOX 256 • CHEROKEE, N. C.
ISBN 0-935741-05-

MOLLY (Runningwolfe) SEQUOYAH

This book has its source in people like Molly Sequoyah pictured above. She lives in the Big Cove section of the Qualla Boundary in Western North Carolina, and belongs to the Eastern Band of Cherokees. She represents many of the older Indian women in this country who have a rich and interesting background of food and herb gathering, preparation, and use.

Although many of the traditional dishes and formulas have been reduced to recipe form, there are many also that live only in the minds and memories of people like Molly. To her and to many like her we owe our gratitude for helping us to make this book possible.

CONTENTS

INTRODUCTION

(AN ANCIENT INDIAN LEGEND)

Once upon a time, in the beginning days of life upon the earth, man, animals, and plants lived together in equality and mutual helpfulness. Man was one with his environment in a beautiful balance of nature. The needs of all were met in a world of plenty.

Man became quite aggressive, however, in his relationship with the rest of his world and began to care less and less for the rights and privileges of the others. Soon the harmony was disrupted.

Aggressive man was multiplying so rapidly that the other creatures became alarmed and called a meeting of all insects, birds, fishes, reptiles and four-footed beasts. Their hostility having been provoked, they joined forces against man and devised many diseases to slow down in his encroachment upon the earth. The bond between man and the other creatures was broken.

Man found that his aggressive behavior had brought much sickness upon him and had made it hard for him to secure the food he needed. Many methods were devised to appease the spirits of the animals which he killed for food.

The plant life remained friendly to man, however, and when they heard about the many diseases inflicted upon him they responded by offering themselves as cures and remedies for his ailments. Each tree, herb, shrub, grass, and moss devised a cure for man if only he would discover and use it.

Thus man created a situation of struggle and turmoil. To have food and to keep himself healthy, he must consider the hostility of the animals and the friendship of the plant life. He must carefully and prayerfully secure and prepare his meat and plant foods within the difficulties that he himself had devised. Through the years the delicate art of securing and preparing both food and medicines developed among the Indian peoples.

Included in these pages is information designed both to acquaint one with Indian lore and provide usable recipes for enjoyment of Indian foods and medicines.

VeGetable
and
Wild Plant
Foods

VEGETABLES AND WILD PLANT FOODS

Perhaps one of the greatest contributions of the American Indian to mankind is the introduction of new edibles to our diet. More than half of the food enjoyed today is derived from early Indian sources.

A thousand years before Columbus set sail for the ''new world'' the American Indian was already skillfully cultivating and preparing foods that he had tamed from the wilds.

Thousands of years before that, as the nomadic tribes spread across the continent, the men spent much of their time finding and killing wild game to provide their families with food. Women and children canvassed the woodlands and plains seeking and securing plant foods to supplement the diet of meat and to use as cures for their ills.

Gradually as the tribes used the same campsites over and over again, they found edible plant life growing from the seeds that they themselves had cast into the refuse piles long before. An understanding and development of plant cultivation took place over the years until many of the Indian people were not only raising gardens but developing new or improved varieties of plant foods.

Following in this book are many present day possibilities in delicious foods made possible through this long period of ingenious development by the American Indian. Included also is a brief section on the use of wild plants for medicinal purposes.

SELU — THE MOTHER OF CORN

According to an ancient legend of the Cherokees there was a time when corn was provided without work by the magic powers of a woman named SELU.

SELU lived with her hunter husband and two sons in the mountain country. One of the sons was very mischievous, and wondering where his mother got the corn that she brought home each day to grind, he talked his brother into joining him in spying on their mother.

Following their mother secretly, they saw her climb the ladder to the storehouse nearby that stood high above the ground on four poles. Carefully they pulled mud from between the logs until they could watch what she was doing inside. Great was their surprise when they saw their mother set the basket on the floor and shake herself vigorously to have corn fall abundantly from her body into the basket.

Their first thought was that their mother was a witch and must be put to death. Selu, knowing their thoughts, gave them some instructions before killing her. "When you have killed me," she said, "Clear a large piece of ground in front of the house and drag my body seven times around the circle. Then drag me seven times over the ground inside the circle, and stay up all night and watch. In the morning you will have plenty of corn."

The boys followed her instructions, except they cleared the yard only in seven small spots. The corn came up in those spots, and since that time it is only by planting, hard work and prayers to Selu that corn can be obtained, and even then it grows only in certain spots across the land.

8

LEATHER BRITCHES
Makes 4-6 servings

1 pound green beans, washed
2 quarts water
1/4 pound salt pork, diced

2 teaspoons salt
1/8 teaspoon fresh ground pepper

Snap the ends off the beans, and string on heavy thread. Hang in sunny place to dry for two months. When you are ready to cook the beans, soak them for 1 hour in the two quarts of water. Add the salt pork, salt and pepper, and bring to a boil. Reduce heat and simmer very slowly, stirring occasionally, for 3 hours. Add additional water if necessary. Serve hot, with lots of broth, as a vegetable. Corn pone is the perfect accompaniment — good for "sopping up" the potlikker.

(Note: This recipe takes two months to prepare)

BAKED CUCUMBERS
Makes 4-6 servings

4 cucumbers, peeled and quartered
** lengthwise**
2 tablespoons butter or margarine

1 teaspoon dill seed, crushed
1/4 teaspoon fresh ground pepper
1 teaspoon salt

Place a layer of cucumbers in the bottom of an 8''x 8''x 2'' baking dish and dot with half of the butter or margarine. Mix together the seasonings, and sprinkle half over the layer of cucumbers. Add a second layer of cucumbers, dot with butter, and sprinkle with remaining seasonings. Bake, uncovered, in a hot oven, 400°F., for 1 hour. Stir cucumbers lightly once, pushing the top layers to the bottom and lifting the bottom cucumbers to the top. Serve hot.

MOHAWK INDIAN CORN

1 can whole kernel corn
1 small package black walnuts

1/2 teaspoon black walnut flavoring
2 tablespoons butter

Empty a can of corn packed in water (not creamed corn) into a pot. Add sufficient water and heat, also adding a small package of black walnuts. Then add about 1/2 teaspoon of black walnut flavoring which is available at most grocery stores. Heat with 2 tablespoons butter and serve.

CHEROKEE BEAN BALLS
Makes 8 servings

2 cups brown beans
4 cups cornmeal

1/2 cup flour
1 teaspoon soda

Boil beans in plain water until tender. Put cornmeal, flour and soda in large mixing bowl. Mix well. Add boiling beans and some of the juice to the cornmeal mixture to form a stiff dough. Roll in balls and drop in pot of boiling hot water. Let cook for 30 minutes at slow boil.

10

SWEET POTATO CAKES
Makes 10-12 servings

4 large sweet potatoes
3 eggs
1-1/2 teaspoons salt

1/8 teaspoon fresh ground pepper
1 tablespoon cooking oil

Parboil the potatoes until tender; peel and mash them. Mix in the eggs, salt, and pepper. Heat the oil on a large griddle until a drop of water sizzles; drop the potato batter from a large spoon, and brown on both sides. As you turn the pancakes flatten them with a spatula slightly. Add more oil to the griddle as needed. This recipe will make about 15 cakes about 3'' in diameter. Serve hot with butter and, if you like, honey.

BAKED PUMPKIN
Makes 6-8 servings

1 small pumpkin
2 tablespoons apple cider

2 tablespoons honey
2 tablespoons melted butter
or margarine

Wash the pumpkin well, place on a pie pan, and bake in a moderate oven, 350°F., for 1-1/2 hours. Remove from the oven and cut a hole in the top of the pumpkin about 3'' to 4'' in diameter. Scoop out pulp and seeds. Mix together the honey, cider, and melted butter or margarine. Baste the mixture over the flesh of the pumpkin. Replace top, return to moderate oven and continue to bake for 35 to 40 minutes longer, basting occasionally. Serve whole, scooping out the individual portions at the table, or cut into wedges as you would a melon. Ladle a little of the cider mixture over each serving.

BATTER-FRIED SQUASH BLOSSOMS
Makes 8 servings

Squash blossoms, picked as they
  are just about to open (2-3 doz.)
1 cup milk
1/2 cup cooking oil

1 tablespoon flour
1/8 teaspoon fresh ground pepper
1 teaspoon salt
Paprika (garnish)

In a shaker jar, combine milk, flour, salt and pepper. Place squash blossoms in large pan and gently pour the milk-flour mixture over them. Heat the oil in a large heavy skillet until a drop of water will sizzle. Fry the batter-coated blossoms in the hot oil until golden brown, drain on paper toweling and sprinkle with paprika. Serve hot.

FRIED HOMINY
Makes 6-8 servings

6 strips bacon cut into pieces
1/8 teaspoon pepper
1/2 teaspoon salt

2 pounds drained hominy
2 scallions sliced thin (include tops)

Fry the bacon in a large, heavy skillet until brown and crisp. Stir in hominy and salt, stirring, for 5 minutes. Add pepper, and scallions, stirring for 5 minutes more.

BAKED SWEET POTATOES
AND HICKORY NUT SAUCE
Makes 4 servings

1 cup hickory nuts **6-8 baking sweet potatoes**
3 cups water **Sugar to taste**

Prepare hickory nuts a day ahead of time as follows: Beat 1 cup
nut meat until it forms butter as in peanut butter. Roll into a ball
and place in refrigerator. The next day bake 6 or 8 baking potatoes
until done. Peel off skins and place in serving bowl. Then put nut
balls in a sieve and place in quart size bowl. Pour about 3 cups
scalding water over ball and stir until it has completely melted. Add
enough sugar to taste and pour over sweet potatoes and serve.

CACTUS SALAD
Makes 4 servings

1 — 7-1/4 oz. can natural cactus **1 — 7 oz. can pimiento, drained**
**   in salt water, drained**

Dressing

3 tablespoons salad oil **2 tablespoons**
1 scallion, washed and minced **   tarragon vinegar**
1 clove garlic, peeled and crushed **1/8 teaspoon fresh ground pepper**

Arrange a bed of cactus on a small platter. Slice the pimiento into
julienne strips and place over the cactus. Mix together the dressing
ingredients and pour over salad. Marinate in the refrigerator an hour
before serving.

WILD MEAT FOODS
ANIMAL, FOWL, & FISH

KANATI — THE ORIGIN OF GAME HUNTING

Hunting was unnecessary many years ago shortly after the world was created. The story of Kanati explains the origin of hunting and trapping wild game.

Kanati and his wife Selu had two sons. One of them was born to them naturally but the other was a "Wild-Boy" who sprang from the blood of the deer where Selu washed the meat in the edge of the river. He was wild of eye and had an untamed spirit. Often he would do things that were impossible to humans, and enjoyed using his magical powers in mischievous ways.

One day when Kanati, their father came in with a fat buck and a couple of wild turkeys, the Wild-Boy said to his brother, "I wonder where our father finds so much wild game every time he goes out. Let's wait until he leaves again, and we will follow him into the forest and find out his secret for always returning with good meat for us to eat."

In a few days Kanati arose early and taking his bow he headed into the woods. The rays of the morning sun filtered through the giant trees overhead and fell in gentle patches on the forest floor. Kanati loved the forest, and enjoying the walk he failed to notice the two boys following close behind. At times the Wild-Boy would turn himself into a puff of bird's down and ride unnoticed on Kanati's shoulder, then changing into a boy again he would rejoin his brother on the trail. Following their father deep into the forest they watched carefully from behind some trees.

Kanati, having stopped beside a big rock, rolled it aside, exposing the entrance to a large cave, and much to the surprise of the two boys a buck ran out. Kanati shot it with his bow and arrow, and quickly rolled the stone back over the entrance to the cave. Lifting the buck onto his back he promptly headed back through the forest towards home.

"Oho!" exclaimed the boys from their position behind the trees, "He has all the deer shut up in that hole, and whenever he wants meat he just lets one out and kills it." Thrilled over their discovery of Kanati's secret the boys hurried home, arriving there before their father who had the heavy buck to carry.

A few days later, at the suggestion of the Wild One, the two brothers slipped away from home and were soon standing beside the huge rock that sealed the cave. Rolling the rock away from the entrance, they jumped back as a deer ran out. Just as they were raising their bow to shoot it another ran out, and then another and another until the boys became so confused, and excited that they simply stood back in amazement and unbelief. After numberless deer had bounded from the cave and disappeared into the density of the forest, droves of raccoons, rabbits and other animals came forth and scurried into the underbrush. Last came great flocks of turkeys, pigeons, partridges and other birds that darkened the sky like a cloud and made a great noise with the beating of their wings in flight.

Kanati, sitting at home, heard the sound like distant thunder on the mountains and knew right away that his boys were up to no good again. Hurrying from the house, he went up the mountain in the direction of the noise. Soon he stood by the cave where he kept the game and found the two boys standing by the rock. All the animals and birds were gone, Kanati was furious, and before he spoke at all he went into the cave and kicked the covers off four jars in the corner, when out swarmed bedbugs, fleas, lice, and gnats which got all over the boys. They screamed with pain and fright, until Kanati, thinking that they had been punished enough, knocked the vermin off of them and scolded them harshly.

"Now, you rascals," he said, "You have always had plenty of meat to eat and never had to work at all for

it. When you were hungry, I simply came up here and got a deer or turkey and brought it home for your mother to cook. Now since you have let all the animals escape you will have to work hard for your food. When you want meat, you will have to search the forest, walking far and sometimes returning with nothing. Go home now to your mother while I see if I can find us something to eat for supper.

Thus the hunting and killing of game has been a task of great skill and hard work during the long history of the Indian people.

CHARCOAL-BROILED BUFFALO STEAKS

Buffalo Steaks (unfrozen) 1" thick **Pepper**
Salt   **Other spices or seasoning to taste**

Broil the steaks on a grill or in a broiling rack about 3 inches from
red coals as you would a beef steak. Season with salt and pepper
and add your favorite meat sauce.

SQUIRREL-COUNTRY STYLE

2 Squirrels   **Flour to dredge**
Salt to taste   **6 tablespoons fat**
Pepper to taste   **2 cups water**

Cut squirrel into serving pieces and shake in a paper bag containing
seasoned flour to dredge well. Fry in skillet until golden brown. Remove squirrel from skillet and pour off all grease except 2 tablespoons.
Add water and bring to a boil. Return squirrel to skillet; turn to low
heat, cover, and cook for about 1 hour, until meat leaves bone.

OLD FASHION SQUIRREL STEW

Salt and pepper squirrel to taste. Boil in water until very, very tender.
Debone. Take 1/2 cup of cooled liquid in which the squirrel was
cooked and make dumplings with self-rising flour. Put deboned squirrel
back in broth and add cut strips of dumplings to broth and squirrel
while cooking. Add a little butter; and if you wish, you may drop
three or four eggs into this mixture. Do not stir until eggs are done.
(You may add about 1/2 cup of sweet milk to the dumplings before
adding eggs if you wish.)

APACHE FRIED RABBIT (WILD)

Makes 4 servings

Dress swamp or cotton-tail rabbit. Wash, cut up, cover with water. Cook until about done. Take pieces out of liquid, dust with flour, salt and fry brown in a skillet of pork-fat.

VENISON AND WILD RICE STEW

Makes 6-8 servings

3-1/2 pounds shoulder of venison, cut into 2'' cubes

2 teaspoons salt

1/8 teaspoon fresh ground pepper

2 quarts water

2 yellow onions, peeled and quartered

1-1/2 cups wild rice, washed in cold water

Place the venison, water, and onions in a large, heavy kettle, and simmer uncovered, for 3 hours or until venison is tender. Mix in the salt, pepper, and wild rice, cover and simmer for 20 minutes. Stir in mixture, then simmer, uncovered for about 20 minutes more or until rice is tender and most of the liquid absorbed.

BATTER FRIED FROG LEGS

Makes 4-6 servings

1 egg beaten

1/2 teaspoon salt

2 pounds frog legs

1/2 cup corn meal

1/8 teaspoon pepper

1/2 cup cooking oil

Mix the egg, corn meal, salt, and pepper together to form a batter. Dip the frog legs into the batter, then fry in the oil in a large, heavy skillet for 25 minutes, turning so that they brown evenly on all sides.

CRISPY FRIED FISH

Makes 4-6 servings

2 pounds small dressed fish
1-1/2 teaspoons salt
Dash pepper
Fat or oil for frying

1/4 cup milk
1/2 cup flour
1/4 cup cornmeal

Thaw frozen fish, clean, wash and dry fish. Add salt and pepper to milk. Mix flour and corn meal. Dip fish in milk and roll in flour mixture. Fry in hot fat at moderate heat for 4 to 5 minutes or until brown on one side. Turn carefully and fry 4 to 5 minutes longer until other side is brown and fish flakes easily when tested with a fork. Drain on paper.

OCTOPUS FRITTERS

Makes 8 servings

2 small octopus weighing about
 1-1/2 pounds each, cleaned
1 teaspoon salt
1/3 cup cooking oil

2 yellow onions, peeled
 and minced
2 eggs
1 cup flour

Drop the octopus into a large kettle of rapidly boiling water and boil, uncovered, for 20 minutes. Drain and plunge into ice water. Using a coarse brush, scrape away the purple skin. Cut off the legs and chop fine. Discard the head. Mix together the onions, salt, eggs and flour to form a batter. Then stir in the minced octopus. Shape into flat cakes about 3'' in diameter. Heat the oil in a large, heavy skillet, and brown the octopus fritters well on each side. Serve hot with butter.

IROQUOIS FISH SOUP

Boil fish of any kind in a pot with a quantity of water. If fish was not fillet, remove bones. Stir in coarse corn siftings (coarse corn meal) to make a soup of suitable consistency. If wild onions and greens are available toss them into the soup pot to add both color and flavor.

ROAST PHEASANT STUFFED WITH GRAPES AND NUTS

Makes 4 servings

3 lbs. pheasant, dressed and larded
1/2 teaspoon thyme
1 tablespoon salt
1/8 teaspoon fresh ground pepper

3/4 cup butter
18 dried juniper berries, crushed
1 cup mixed broken nut meats
(walnuts or any kind)

Remove any pinfeathers from the birds and singe off hairs. Melt the butter and mix in thyme, salt, crushed juniper berries, and pepper. Rub the birds well inside and out with the seasoned butter. Mash half of the grapes, then mix with remaining seasoned butter. Stuff each bird very full, skewer openings shut, and truss. Wrap remaining stuffing in aluminum foil. Place birds on a rack in an open roasting pan and roast in a very hot oven, 425°F., for 15 minutes. The foil wrapped stuffing can be placed in the roasting pan beside the birds. Baste with drippings, reduce heat to moderate, 350°F., and continue to roast for 30 minutes more or until birds are tender, baste every 10 minutes with drippings.

INDIAN BEVERAGES SOUPS & BROTHS

A GIFT FROM HEAVEN

LEGEND OF THE "SUN-FLUID" — "TSO-CI"

An old Indian woman of ancient times was said to have cut a rent in the sky through which poured the most delicious and satisfying liquid. The sun then explained to the woman how to prepare and use the liquid. It thus became known as TSO-CI, meaning "sun-fluid."

The basis for the liquid was corn, and its use in many forms was found among a great number of the American Indian tribes. Its variations were known by such names as "Sofki" by the Creeks, "Atole" by the Mexicans, "Sagamite" by the French, "Tanbubo" or "Tafula" by

22

Story Teller   V. Stroud
                                SGS '70

the Choctaw, and was known to be used in varying forms also by the Seminole and the Chickasaw.

Using corn, sometimes parched and ground or soaked in lye, as a base, many ingredients were added to give flavor to the beverage or broth. Fresh pork was used as seasoning and often beans, hickory nuts, marrow, wood ashes, or other ingredients were added.

Out of the legendary rent in the sky the sun fluid seemed to flow into Indian food culture in many forms and many places.

Although the corn-drink and water were the most common beverages of the ancient Indian many other drinks were from berries and various teas from roots, bark, twigs, and leaves. Soups and broths were often left to simmer over the fire providing ready enrichment and satisfaction for the family.

NUT AND MINT SOUP

Makes 6-8 servings

**2 — 10-1/2 oz. cans
beef consomme**

1/2 cup raw pinon nuts

Leaves of 2 stalks mint, washed

**2 — 1 lb. 4 oz. cans chick-peas,
drained and rinsed**

3 cups water

Place the consomme, water, and pinon nuts in a large saucepan and bring to a boil. Reduce heat, add chick-peas, and simmer 15 minutes. Turn heat off, add mint leaves, and let steep about a minute. Serve at once, seasoning each helping with fresh ground pepper.

PEANUT SOUP

Makes 6 servings

**1 — 9-1/4 oz. jar, dry roasted
peanuts**

2 cups water

2 cups milk

**2 — 5.4 gram packages instant
chicken broth**

1 tablespoon minced chives.

Chop the nuts fine, or puree in a blender. Place the nuts and the remaining ingredients in a large saucepan, and heat, stirring for 5 to 20 minutes. Serve hot. Make the portions small—the soup is rich.

APACHE ACORN STEW

Makes 6 servings

**2-1/2–3 pounds round steak
Sweet Acrons
(enough to make 3/4 cups
of acorn flour)**

**Salt
Wooden or plastic bowl**

Cut the round steak into small bite-size pieces and cook in about one quart of water. Let it simmer for about three hours or until meat is well done. Salt to taste. Shell the sweet acrons and grind them into very fine flour until you have about 3/4 cup of flour. Strain the broth from the meat (it will be used later). Shred the meat and placing it in a wooden or plastic bowl mix it with the acorn flour (aluminum discolors the flour). Pour the hot broth over this mixture and stir. It is now ready to serve in individual bowls. Often times fry bread is served with this stew.

YELLOWJACKET SOUP

Although the mention of "yellowjacket soup" immediately raises an eyebrow on those unaccustomed to such a food, it was actually a delicacy and should not be criticized until tried. Only the bravest dare venture into the preparation of this exotic Eastern Indian food.

Secure an entire nest of ground-dwelling yellowjackets when it is full of grubs. Loosen all the uncovered grubs by heating and remove them. Heat the nest with the remaining grubs over a fire until the thin paper-like covering parches. Pick out the yellowjackets and brown them over the fire. Cook the browned yellowjackets in boiling water to make soup and season to taste.

Good luck and good eating!!

YAUPON TEA

Makes 6-8 servings

1/3 cup dried yaupon leaves   **1 quart water**

Place the yaupon leaves and water in a saucepan and boil for 15 minutes. Strain and serve.

MINT TEA

Makes 2 quarts

10 large stalks fresh mint, washed   **2 quarts water**

Place mint and water in a large saucepan, and bring slowly to a boil. Turn off heat, cover, and let steep for 5 minutes. Strain and serve.

HONEY DRINK

Makes about 1 quart

1 quart water   **2/3 cup honey**

Place water and honey in a large jar with a close-fitting lid, and shake well to blend ingredients. Chill thoroughly, and serve iced in small glasses.

SASSAFRAS TEA

Make 1-1/2 quarts

4 sassafras roots, each   **1-1/2 quarts water**
about 2'' long

Scrub the roots well with a stiff brush, rinse, and scrape away the bark. Place roots and bark scrapings along with the water in a large saucepan. Bring slowly to a boil, reduce heat, and simmer together gently for 15 minutes. Turn off heat, and let tea steep for 10 minutes. Strain and serve.

JUNIPER OR SPICE WOOD TEA

Makes 1 quart

20 tender young sprigs of juniper   **2 quarts water**
or spicewood, washed

Place the sprigs and water in a large saucepan, bring to boil, cover, reduce heat, and let simmer gently for 15 minutes. Turn heat off and let tea steep for 10 minutes. Strain and serve. Sweeten if desired.

INDIAN CHESTNUT BREAD

Makes 5-6 servings

Peel one pound of chestnuts and scale to take off the inside skin. Add enough corn meal to hold chestnuts together, mixing chestnuts and cornmeal with boiling water. Wrap in green fodder or green corn shucks, tying each bun securely with white twine. Place in a pot of boiling water and cook until done. Salt when eating if desired. Bean bread can be made the same way, but cook beans until tender before adding corn meal. No salt should be added before or during cooking or the bread will crumble.

CHEROKEE HUCKLEBERRY BREAD

2 cups self-rising flour	1 egg
1 cup sugar	1 stick butter
1 cup milk	1 teaspoon vanilla extract
2 cups berries (huckleberries or blueberries)	

Cream eggs, butter, and sugar together. Add flour, milk, and vanilla. Sprinkle flour on berries to prevent them from going to the bottom. Add berries to mixture. Put in baking pan and bake in oven at 350°F. Approx. 40 minutes or until done.

CHEROKEE YAM CAKES

Makes 18 3'' cakes

2 cups sifted flour
1-1/2 teaspoons sugar
1-1/2 teaspoons salt

2-1/2 teaspoons baking powder
1/2 cup salad oil
1/2 cup milk

1 cup mashed yams or sweet potatoes. Sift flour, baking powder, sugar and salt into a bowl. Pour oil and milk into a measuring cup but do not stir. Add to yams. Blend well. Add to flour mixture and mix lightly with a fork until mixture holds together. Turn dough out onto a floured surface and knead gently until smooth, about 12 kneading strokes. Roll dough about 1/4'' thick and cut into rounds with floured biscuit cutter. Place rounds on a baking sheet. Bake at 425°F. for 10-20 minutes. Serve hot, or split when cold and toast.

BANAHA CHOCTAW-CORN SHUCK BREAD

6 cups corn meal

2 teaspoons soda

Pour enough boiling water over the meal-soda mixture to make a soft dough which can be handled with the hands. Prepare 4 to 6 handfuls of corn shucks by pouring boiling water over them to cover, then strip a few shucks to make strings. Tie 2 strips together at ends. Lay an oval shaped ball of dough on shucks. Fold carefully around dough and tie in the middle with the strings. Place in large stew pot and boil 30 to 45 minutes.

SQUAW BREAD

Prepare dough using 2 cups flour, 1/2 teaspoon baking powder, 1 teaspoon salt, and sufficient amount of milk. Divide the dough into parts, and shape each into a round pone about the size of your skillet and 1/8'' thick. Fry the bread in about 1/4'' hot cooking oil quickly until golden brown on each side. Cut into wedges and serve hot. Delicious with butter, jams or other sweet spreads.

HERBS
AND
THEIR USES

HERBS & MEDICINE

All day the young Indian boy had been standing out on top of a high mountain meadow looking at the sun. He had not taken his eyes away from that burning orb since it first rose above the brim of the distant peaks. In back of him sat an old man who watched the boy as carefully as the boy watched the sun. Occasionally the old one made passes over a round pottery vessel that contained a combination of many herbs. These herbs were the old man's medicine for the boy. The boy was his, so to speak; he had been given to the old man when he was a small baby and the old one had raised him as a medicine man. He was now in the process of giving the boy the final training that would allow him the full privileges and rank of medicine man. All the young boy's life, he had been in training for work he would soon be doing. It had started long before he could recall. The women he was turned over to for the first years of his life had been given detailed orders about the things he would be allowed to do and the things he must not. He was never allowed to play as ordinary children played. He was taught from the first to lie still and not to cry. Then to listen and not talk, and last when his mind began to work he was taught to remember and not to forget. He spent endless hours by the side of the old man listening to stories about the past of the great Indians and about the things to come. He tended the sacred fire for weeks at a time and sat without moving until at times the bones of his body grew stiff and cold. Always after listening to the stories of how the world came to be and how all things were made and why these things were, the old man made the boy repeat them until they were right in his mind. The training went on all the time, from the early morning until the council fire was allowed to burn down to live ashes at night.

Such was the preparation of a boy's life who would one day be a Medicine Man. The place and ritual differed in different tribes and areas of the continent, but to most tribes the gathering and preparation of herbs for medicines was entrusted to the skills of the well-trained few.

Through many centuries of gathering and use, the art of herbal-medicine became sophisticated and effective as a means of caring for the health needs of the tribe.

Interestingly enough we are now living in an age which places strong emphasis upon the return to natural foods and remedies. Perhaps we are on the edge of rediscovering an art long known and used by those who considered the plant world their friends.

HERB & PLANT USES

The following list is provided simply to acquaint the reader with some of the plants and their uses according to ancient records. No claim is made for their effectiveness or lack of it in today's world.

PLANT	PART	USE
Dandelion	roots	chest pain
Gum plant	leaves	sores on horses
Jalap	roots	purgative
Jimson weed	seeds	were sacred
Mandrake	plant boiled	insecticide
Prickly ash	root-bark	colic
New Jersey tea	root-tea	bowel trouble
Jack-in-the-pulpit	corm	muscular pain
Blue vervain	leaves boiled	stomach ache
Boneset	leaf-tea	colds, fever
Yellow root	root-tea	sore mouth, throat
Cascara Sagrada	bark-tea	laxative
Dogwood	bark-tea	fevers, colds
Elder	bark-tea	heartburn
Peach leaves	leaf poultice	boils
Cat-tail	root poultice	sores
Hoary willow	inner bark-tea	cough
Red cedar	leaves, berries	headache
White oak	root, bark-tea	diarrhea
Moonwart	bruised roots	cuts
Red alder	bark-tea	high blood
Green Hellebore	ground roots	hernia
Ground Ivy	leaf-tea	hives
Ginseng	root-tea	colic
Spignet	root-tea	backache
Wild cherry	bark-tea	measles
Bull nettle	root necklace	baby-teething